# The Mysterious World of

# Microorganisms

### Written by
### Isabel Thomas

## Contents

## Collins

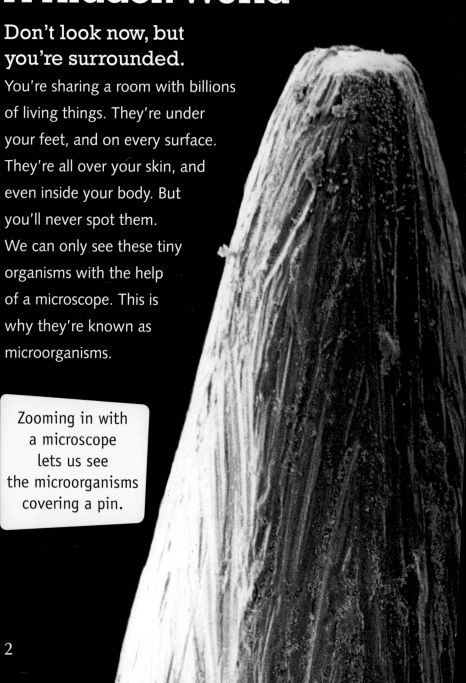

# A Hidden World

## Don't look now, but you're surrounded.

You're sharing a room with billions of living things. They're under your feet, and on every surface. They're all over your skin, and even inside your body. But you'll never spot them. We can only see these tiny organisms with the help of a microscope. This is why they're known as microorganisms.

Zooming in with a microscope lets us see the microorganisms covering a pin.

## Helpful or harmful?

Like all living things, microorganisms spend their time moving, feeding, growing and **reproducing**. When they do this inside plants and animals, some cause harm. These are the "germs" that hit the headlines and give microorganisms a bad name. More often, microorganisms help plants and animals, including humans. In fact, we couldn't survive without them.

These microorganisms are single-celled algae.

# MOST WANTED

**Antoine Van Leeuwenhoek (1632–1723)**

Before microscopes were invented 400 years ago, no one had a clue that squillions of microorganisms call our planet home. Since then, people have made world-changing discoveries about the secret lives of these tiny living things. These doctors, nurses and scientists are the microorganisms' most-wanted. In the 1670s, Antoine van Leeuwenhoek began making his own microscopes. He was the first person to spot bacteria and a tiny fungus called yeast.

3

# A Spotter's Guide

Microscopes are bigger and better than they were in the 1600s, and almost 200,000 different types of microorganisms have been spotted so far. To help keep track of all these microorganisms, scientists put them into groups. Living things with similar features are put into the same group. This is called classification.

**Plants**

**Fungi**

Around 120,000 types of fungi have been discovered. Some – such as mushrooms – are large and look like plants. Others are tiny microorganisms, with just one cell.

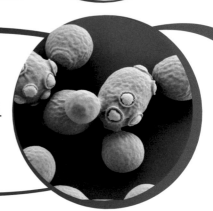

**Bacteria**

These tiny living things are made up of just one cell. Around 7,000 types have been named so far.

There are five main groups of living things – animals, plants, bacteria, fungi and protists. These groups are also known as kingdoms. Just as there are many different types of plants and animals, there are many different types of bacteria, fungi and protists.

**Animals**

The different kingdoms can be thought of as different branches on a "tree of life".

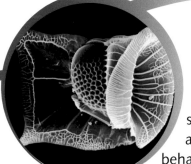

**Protists**
This kingdom is where scientists put tiny living things that don't fit in any other kingdom! The 13,000 different protists are all sorts of shapes and sizes. Some act like animals. Others behave more like plants.

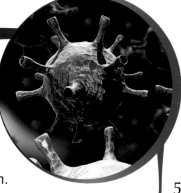

**Viruses**
Viruses are the smallest, simplest microorganisms. Almost 3,000 types have been named so far. Scientists aren't sure if they count as living things or not, so they don't have a kingdom of their own.

5

# Bacteria

Bacteria were some of the very first living things on the planet. They've been calling Earth home for more than 3.5 billion years, while the first animals appeared just 2.5 to 1.5 billion years ago. The first bacteria seen under a microscope were rod-shaped. They were named "bacteria" after the Greek word for "little stick".

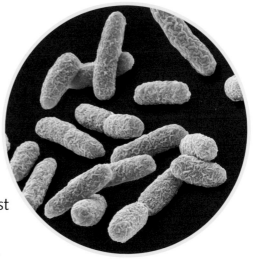

Bacteria can also be shaped like balls, commas and spirals.

## How micro are bacteria?

Living things are made up of **cells** – tiny units that can do one or more jobs. It takes billions or trillions of cells to build a plant or animal – all working together to help the plant or animal move, feed, grow and reproduce. In contrast, each bacterium is just one cell big. It has to move, feed, grow and reproduce on its own!

 MICRO STATS

37 trillion: Number of cells that make up your body
1: Number of cells that make up a bacterium

The smallest bacteria are less than a millionth of a metre long – you could line a thousand of them up on this full stop. The biggest bacteria can grow up to half a millimetre long, but giants like this are rare.

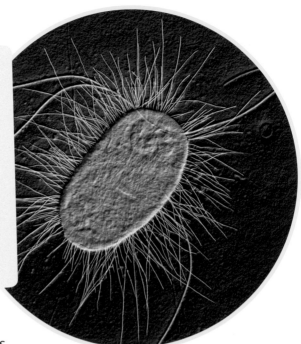

Some bacteria have tails called **flagella** for moving around.

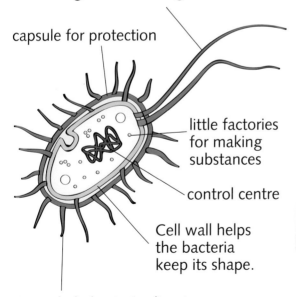

capsule for protection

little factories for making substances

control centre

Cell wall helps the bacteria keep its shape.

Hairs help bacteria cling to each other – or surfaces.

This is what a bacteria cell looks like inside. It's more complex than one of your cells – not surprising, as the bacterium has to survive on its own!

# How bacteria feed

Just like plants and animals, bacteria need to feed. They need energy and **nutrients** to survive and grow. Most bacteria get these things by **absorbing** food through their cell walls. Only tiny particles of food can make it through the cell wall. Unless they're lucky enough to be swimming in sugar, most bacteria have to break down their food before they can eat it.

They do this by releasing special chemicals through their cell walls. These chemicals do the same job as the ones in your digestive system. They break up the food into pieces tiny enough to pass into the bacteria.

The pink and yellow objects are bacteria, feeding on a piece of cucumber on a compost heap.

## What's on the menu?

Bacteria aren't fussy – think of almost any substance, and you'll find a type of bacteria that can break it down and use it as food:

Sugar ✓   Dead animals ✓   Sewage ✓

Crude oil ✓   Toxic waste ✓

This is why bacteria are found EVERYWHERE – in soil, stones and air; in shallow ponds and deep oceans; in boiling volcanoes and Antarctic ice. Bacteria also live on or inside every other living thing – including us!

Bacteria are even breaking down the steel hull of the wrecked *Titanic*!

9

## The body biome

You're not just an animal – you're a walking Eden Project, a home for trillions of microorganisms. Most of these are bacteria.

Bacteria hitch a ride in our noses, mouths and elsewhere!

## Garden in your gut

Your digestive system is the perfect habitat for bacteria – warm, dark and full of food. Any bacteria tough enough to survive a bath in your stomach acid can move in. Most of these gut bacteria are helpful. In return for a place to live, they help break down food, so we can absorb it. Some of them build nutrients that we need to survive.

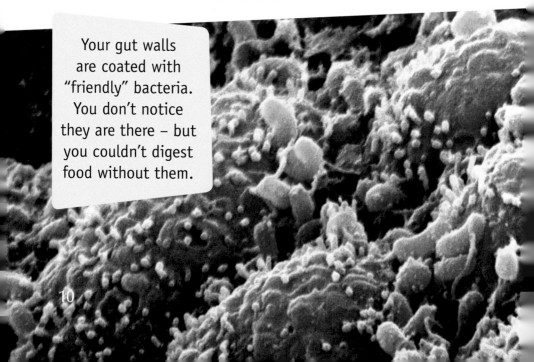

Your gut walls are coated with "friendly" bacteria. You don't notice they are there – but you couldn't digest food without them.

Most animals have helpful bacteria in their guts. Bacteria help to keep bees and their honey healthy, by fighting off any "bad" microorganisms that try to move in.

## MOST WANTED

**Sergei Winogradsky (1856–1953)**

Sergei Winogradsky discovered that bacteria in the soil help plants to get nutrients they wouldn't be able to get on their own. He showed that certain bacteria can grab nitrogen from the air, and turn it into a substance that plants can absorb. Nitrogen is one of the most important nutrients for all living things. In return for making a useful form of nitrogen, the bacteria get some of the food made by the plant.

# Bacterial baddies

Not all types of bacteria can live in our bodies without harming us. Some cause diseases, from ear infections and pneumonia to food poisoning. Even "good" bacteria may cause **symptoms** of disease when they move to the "wrong" part of our body. A harmful invasion of our body by microorganisms is called an infection.

Bacteria can harm our bodies in different ways. Some bacteria attack our cells directly, using them as food. Others produce toxic substances that damage our bodies. One of the most harmful is botulism toxin, produced by *Clostridum botulinum* bacteria. If these bacteria get inside a person, the toxin attacks the nerves and brain. It can paralyse the muscles that control breathing.

These *Clostridium botulinum* bacteria usually live in soil, or mud at the bottom of rivers and oceans. They can produce one of the world's most powerful poisons.

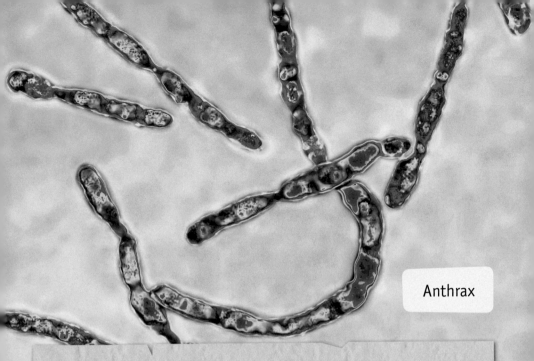

Anthrax

# MOST WANTED

**Robert Koch**
**(1843–1910)**

For thousands of years, people thought that diseases were spread by bad smells. Even after microorganisms were discovered, it was hard to believe something so tiny could harm or kill humans. In the mid-1800s, Louis Pasteur proved living germs really were to blame. Later, Robert Koch found a way to link diseases to particular microorganisms – starting with deadly anthrax. This was the first step in learning how to fight them.

13

# Tooth decay

Your mouth is a like a bacteria safari park. Up to 300 different types of bacteria are in there right now, waiting for their next meal. But it's not the bacteria themselves that attack your teeth – it's their toxic waste.

**MICRO STATS**

People in the world:
**7.2 billion**
Microorganisms in your mouth:
**20 billion**

Some of the bacteria in your mouth glue themselves to your teeth, in clumps of sticky **plaque**. These bacteria feed on the **carbohydrates** in your food. Sugar is their favourite snack, as it's easiest to digest.

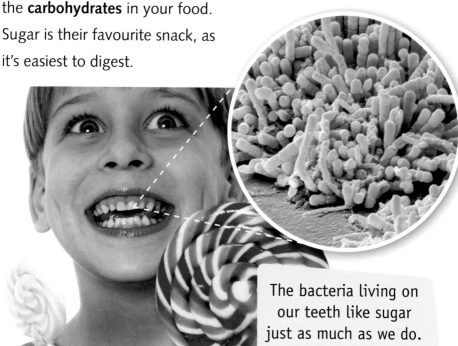

The bacteria living on our teeth like sugar just as much as we do.

Acid made by bacteria has dissolved the **enamel**, causing tooth decay

As holes get close to the centre of the teeth, they become painful

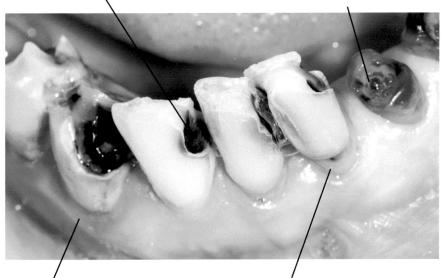

Different substances made by bacteria make gums pink and sore

The gums start to come away from the teeth. This is called gum disease.

Brush your teeth twice a day to scrape away plaque, and stop bacteria making enough acid to dissolve the surface of your teeth.

As plaque bacteria digest their food, they produce acids. These are substances that can dissolve your teeth. Gaps between meals give your saliva a chance to wash away the acid, and repair the damage. But if you eat sugary foods between meals, the bacteria never stop producing acid and your saliva can't keep up.

15

# Deadly bacteria

One or two bad bacteria can't do much harm on their own. The problem comes when millions or billions set up home in our bodies at the same time. Bacteria can reproduce incredibly quickly – they just split in two. Every time this happens, the **population** of bacteria doubles. Some bacteria – such as E. coli – can double in number every hour or less!

# Food poisoning

There are many types of E. coli bacteria. Some live in our intestines and do no harm. Others are famous for causing food poisoning. They do this by making a nasty toxin (poison) that gives people stomach cramps, diarrhea and vomiting.

There are thousands of different ways for E. coli to get into your body (e.g. by touching a farm animal and putting your hands in your mouth, or by eating meat that hasn't been properly cooked). The best way to protect yourself is by washing your hands before touching your mouth.

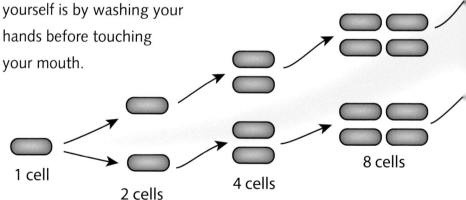

1 cell

2 cells

4 cells

8 cells

# Why haven't bacteria taken over the world?

Bacteria can't keep multiplying in the same place forever. Any habitat – from a plant pot to a person – has a limited amount of food and space. When bacteria run out of food and space, their numbers stabilize and eventually fall. To get more food and space, the best thing for bacteria to do is to move to a new habitat – such as someone else's body! Some bacteria cause symptoms such as coughing, sneezing, diarrhea or vomiting, which help infections to spread.

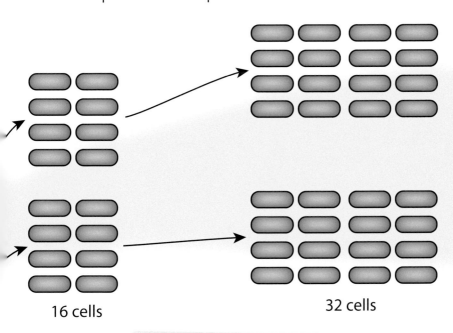

16 cells

32 cells

If the number of E.coli bacteria doubles every hour, one E. coli bacterium can become ten million in just a day!

# Keeping microbes out

Bacteria live everywhere. They're impossible to avoid. But they can't cause an infection unless they attach themselves to (or get inside) the cells of your body. Luckily, your body has lots of ways to keep microorganisms out.

Mucus in your nose, throat and lungs traps microorganisms in the air. The mucus collects at the back of your throat and is swallowed.

Strong stomach acid kills most microorganisms.

Invading microorganisms have to compete for space and food with the huge numbers of friendly bacteria in your intestines. This makes it harder for them to survive.

Slimy mucus stops microorganisms from attaching themselves to the walls of your digestive system.

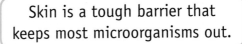

Skin is a tough barrier that keeps most microorganisms out.

Parts of your body without skin are at risk. Tears and saliva contain natural **antiseptics**, to constantly clean your eyes and mouth. You breathe up to 10,000 microorganisms into your lungs every day.

Sweat and skin oils can kill certain microorganisms.

Microorganisms are tiny enough to enter your body through a cut, scratch or burn. To stop this happening, scabs form quickly over damaged skin. This keeps germs out while the skin heals.

19

## The body battlefield

Our bodies have **adapted** over time to keep microorganisms out. But bacteria and other microbes have adaptations that help them find ways in. If microorganisms make it past your body's barriers, your **immune system** takes over. Your immune system is your body's way of fighting invading microorganisms. To do this, it makes special cells called **white blood cells**, which find and kill microorganisms.

## White blood cells

There are two main types of white blood cells. The first type starts working as soon as microorganisms enter the body. When they find one, they wrap themselves around it, kill it, and digest it.

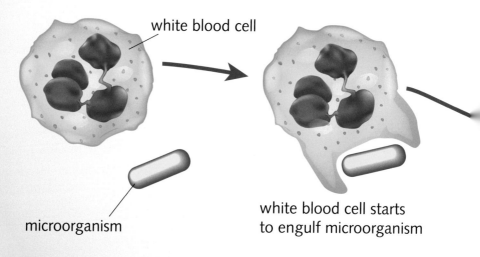

white blood cell

microorganism

white blood cell starts
to engulf microorganism

The second type of white blood cells learns how to recognise particular microorganisms. They carry out targeted attacks, by clinging to the enemy microbe and destroying it. Your immune system targets unfriendly cells, so your own cells and helpful bacteria are not harmed.

## Becoming immune

After your body has beaten an infection, some of the white blood cells that have learnt how to kill that microorganism stay in your blood. If you're infected again, they can start attacking the microorganism more quickly than before. This time, they kill the invaders before you get symptoms. You have become immune to that disease.

White blood cells help to get rid of microorganisms. This helps to protect our immune system from attack.

microorganism is fully surrounded

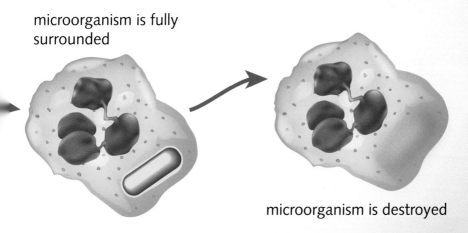

microorganism is destroyed

# Bacteria and decay

Bacteria that live inside plants and animals must adapt to hide from the immune system – or risk being destroyed! **Decomposing** bacteria get around this problem by feeding on dead plants or animals instead. Dead organic material has plenty of substances for microorganisms to feed on. But it no longer has living defence systems, so it won't fight back.

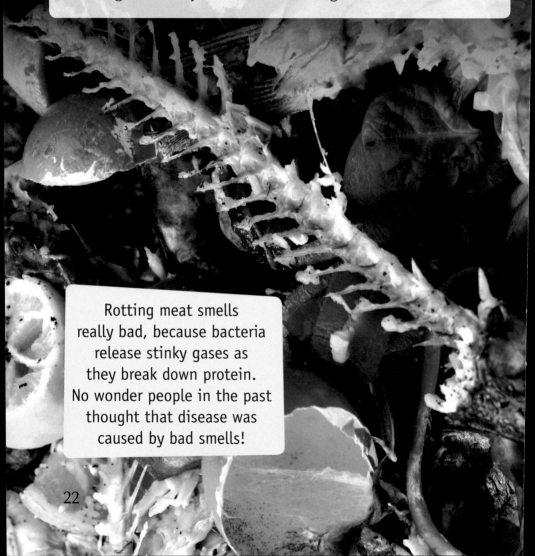

Rotting meat smells really bad, because bacteria release stinky gases as they break down protein. No wonder people in the past thought that disease was caused by bad smells!

## Recycling champions

The breakdown of dead material is called decay. It may seem annoying when it happens to food we were planning to eat, but decay is actually vital for living things. When decomposing bacteria break dead plants and animals down, they release nutrients that can be used by new plants and animals. It's like taking apart an old bike to get the parts you need to build a new one!

# MOST WANTED

**Louis Pasteur
(1822–1895)**

Luckily we can slow down decay, by creating conditions that make it impossible for bacteria to survive. Louis Pasteur was the first to discover that heat kills the microorganisms that cause decay. Today, all the milk we drink is heated after it comes out of the cow, to kill any bacteria living in it. This is called pasteurisation, after Louis himself. Drying, chilling, pickling or sealing food in airtight containers can also slow down decay.

# Fungi

Not all fungi are microorganisms – it's easy to see mushrooms, mildew and **mould** without a microscope. But fungi range in size from the largest living thing on Earth (a mushroom 3.5 miles wide!) to micro-sized yeast, made up of just one cell.

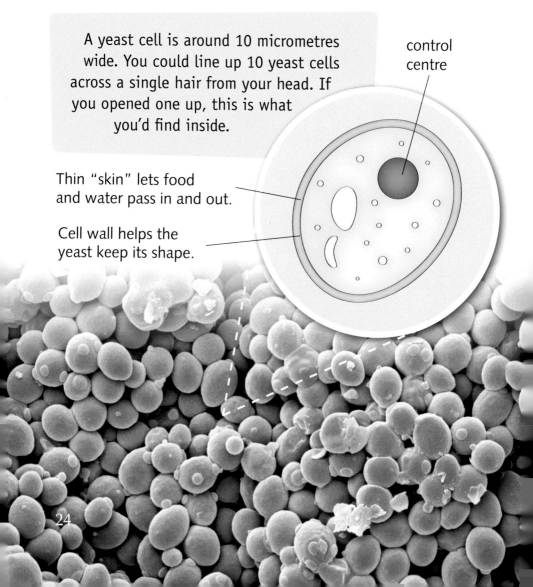

A yeast cell is around 10 micrometres wide. You could line up 10 yeast cells across a single hair from your head. If you opened one up, this is what you'd find inside.

control centre

Thin "skin" lets food and water pass in and out.

Cell wall helps the yeast keep its shape.

# How do fungi feed?

At first glance, many fungi look like plants. But fungi can't make their own food like plants do. Instead, they are parasites that feed on plants and animals – even dead ones!

Dead fruit is a feast for fungus. This mould feeds by breaking down dead material.

Fungi grow anywhere they can find a host (something to feed on). Damp, warm places are best, but some fungi have adapted to cold or dry habitats. You'll find fungi growing on plants, animals, in soil … and even on you!

MICRO
STATS

Fungi in a teaspoon of soil: **120,000**
Bacteria in a teaspoon of soil: **100,000,000**

# A feast for fungi

Fungi don't have mouths or stomachs. Like bacteria, they often feed by releasing chemicals on to the surface they're growing on. These chemicals break up substances – such as carbohydrates – into smaller pieces. The fungus can them absorb these tiny pieces through its cell wall.

This mould is made up of many tiny fungi, busily feeding on the bread

Fungi are really important for breaking down dead wood. Micro-fungi invade logs, helping other **decomposers** to get in.

Fungi like warm, damp places, so food is stored in cool, dry places to try and stop fungi growing.

When fungi feed on a dead plant or animal, they gradually break it down until there is nothing left. This is incredibly useful. Like bacteria, fungi help to **decompose** dead animals and plant. If they didn't, we'd be knee-deep in dead dinosaurs, trees and every other plant and animal that died in the last few billion years!

New animals and plants can use the nutrients that fungi unlock. The materials that make up your body, such as **carbon** and water, may once have been part of a tree that died, and was broken down by fungi.

Decay is not always welcome. Fungi can make food go stale, or even produce toxic waste products that poison humans or animals.

27

## Fungus and disease

A few types of fungi can grow and feed on living plants or animals. Our immune systems can usually zap invading fungi quickly, but sometimes fungi cause infections – especially skin diseases.

## Spread by spores

Athlete's foot spreads easily because the fungi reproduce by making spores. These are tough cells with a protective coat. They can survive on a floor or on a sock for months … until they find another sweaty foot to grow on.

Fungi called dermatophytes love to live in the damp, warm skin between our toes. The sweatier the better! The fungi suck up water, and digest dead skin for food. Unsurprisingly, this makes our skin itchy and dry – a disease known as Athlete's foot.

Fungal spores are everywhere – including millions in your pillow! Some people are allergic to these spores, which causes sneezing and breathing problems.

## Fatal fungi

Fungal skin infections such as Athlete's foot and ringworm are annoying, but not deadly. Spores can cause bigger problems if they start growing in our lungs. This is common in some areas of the world, such as North America, causing diseases such as Valley fever and histoplasmosis. These can be deadly for people with weak immune systems.

MICRO STATS

Types of fungi found so far: **120,000**
Types of fungi that harm people (including poisonous mushrooms and toadstools): **300**

# Infected plants

Plants can get diseases too, and fungi cause most of them. Sometimes these fungi are easy to spot. Sometimes we can only see the damage they've done.

These fungi are parasites – they live on or in plants, taking food but giving nothing back. Fungi can destroy plants, or stop them growing properly. Either way, this is bad news – especially if people are relying on the plants for food.

# Crop killers

Unlike most bacteria, the same fungus can infect many different species of plants. Fungi spread through crops easily. Their spores don't have far to travel in densely planted fields. This is why farmers often spray crops with fungicides.

This mould produces tiny spores that burst into the air. As soon as the spores land in a warm, damp place, they will **germinate**.

# Signs of fungal infection

There are lots of signs that a fungus is living on or in a plant.

Seedlings collapse

Blisters and swellings

Spots on berries

Yellowing leaves

Soft, soggy fruits and vegetables

Spots on leaves or stems

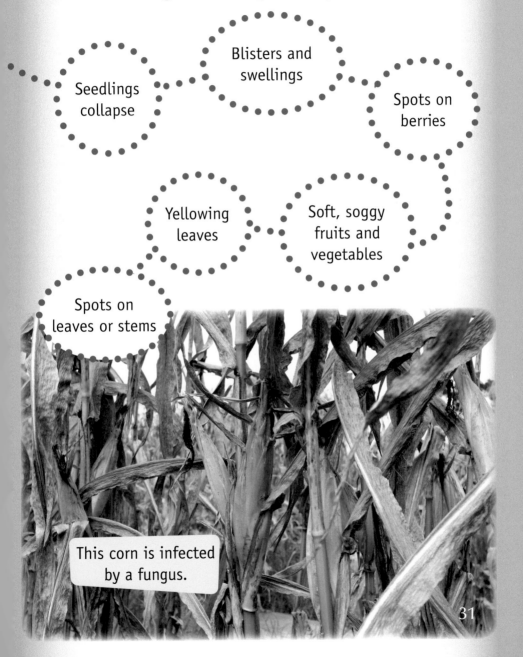

This corn is infected by a fungus.

# Mycorrhizal magic!

Some fungi help the plants they live on. Mycorrhizal fungi and their plant hosts have adapted to live closely together. They help each other survive.

## What are mycorrhizas?

These fungi live on or inside the roots of nine out of every ten plants on Earth. They form a network of tiny strands, growing in and around the roots. This increases the surface area of the roots, helping the plant to suck up more nutrients and water from the soil. Scientists have also found that mycorrhizal fungi help to protect plants against attack from other microorganisms!

Some mycorrhizas wrap themselves around roots, rather than living inside them. Toadstools growing under a tree can be a sign of the huge network of fungi hidden under the ground.

## What do mycorrhizas get in return?

Their food. Fungi can't make their own food, but plants can. Because the fungi live in and around the plants, they can absorb some of the sugars that the plant has made. They don't take enough to harm the plant.

## Why are mycorrhizas so important?

Most wild plants rely on these fungi – they couldn't get the nutrients they need without them. Without the fungi, the plants would die. On land, plants are the producers in most food chains.

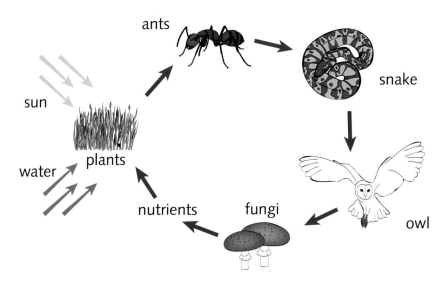

Without plants, most land animals – including humans – would have nothing to eat. (Most sea animals rely on protists rather than plants.)

# Protists

When scientists find a living thing that isn't an animal, plant, fungus or bacteria, they classify it as a protist. This kingdom of living things is very diverse. They feed, move, live and reproduce in many different ways. Some protists have features like miniature animals; others are more like tiny plants.

## Where do protists live?

Protists like wet or moist places, so huge numbers live in rivers, seas and lakes. Zoom in on a drop of seawater or pond water, and you'll find hundreds of protists. They also like damp soil and the watery insides of animals – including us!

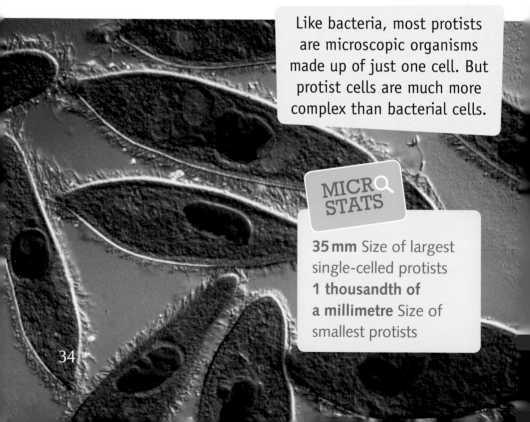

Like bacteria, most protists are microscopic organisms made up of just one cell. But protist cells are much more complex than bacterial cells.

MICRO
STATS

**35 mm** Size of largest single-celled protists
**1 thousandth of a millimetre** Size of smallest protists

Different protists feed, move and reproduce in very different ways.

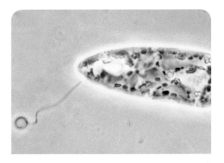

This flagellate swims by whipping its **flagella** from side to side.

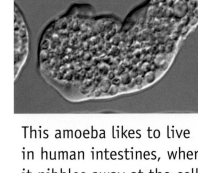

This amoeba likes to live in human intestines, where it nibbles away at the cells that line the gut wall.

The hard, glassy cell walls of these marine protists sink to the seabed when their owners die. Over millions of years, the glassy material forms rocks such as chalk and limestone.

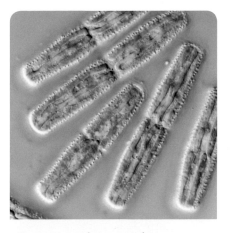

Some protists, such as these green algae, can capture the energy in sunlight and make their own food.

# Protist power!

Algae are the heroes of the protist kingdom. Most algae can make their own food using the energy in sunlight – a trick also carried out by green plants. Many algae are better at this than plants, because they can capture more of the energy in light.

Algae store the food they make as starch. All that stored starch makes algae an important source of food for animals that live in rivers, lakes and oceans. Algae also release oxygen as they make their own food. This is an essential gas for life on Earth. In fact, algae produce most of our planet's food and oxygen!

Protists are a key part of plankton. Other water creatures feed on the plankton. Larger animals eat them, and the energy is passed up the food chain.

**An ocean food chain**

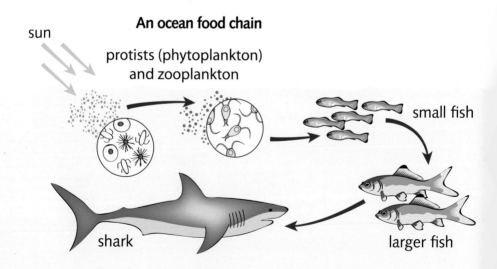

sun

protists (phytoplankton) and zooplankton

small fish

shark

larger fish

These tiny, beautiful algae are called diatoms. There are so many diatoms in the oceans, scientists estimate they capture more energy from sunlight than the world's tropical forests!

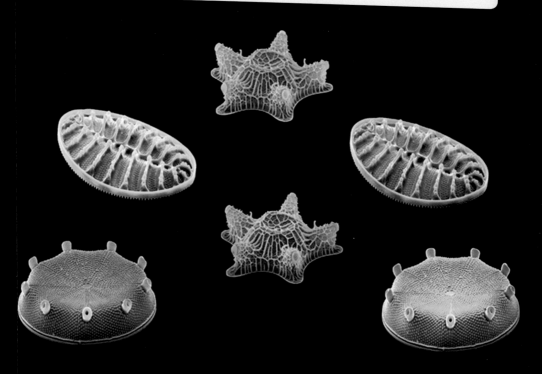

## Marine heroes

Protists are vital for life in seawater habitats. As part of **plankton**, algae and other protists are the main **producers** at the bottom of ocean and freshwater food chains. They are also the main decomposers in the sea, breaking down dead sea animals and plants so the nutrients locked up in their bodies can be recycled.

Cows have adapted to happily munch dung-covered grass. It helps them pick up new micro-sized helpers!

## Protist passengers

You may know that cows have four stomachs, but did you know they are packed with microorganisms, including protists? These microorganisms help cows to digest grass. Most of the nutrients in grass are locked up in a super-tough plant material called cellulose. Cows can't absorb cellulose, and they can't break it down on their own. They need help from protists, bacteria and fungi.

The microorganisms in a cow's gut break chunky cellulose into smaller pieces. This releases energy for the microorganisms. The cow benefits too, because it can absorb the smaller pieces of food. Without the microorganisms, cows would not be able to live on grass. No cows, no milk; no milk, no ice-cream. That's a scary thought!

Cellulose-chomping protists are great when they're digesting grass. Not so great when they're digesting your house! These ones live in the guts of termites. They help the insects to digest wood.

## Protist parasites

Many protists that live inside animals are parasites – taking, but not giving anything back. They can be deadly. Sleeping sickness and malaria are examples of diseases caused by protists setting up home in our bodies.

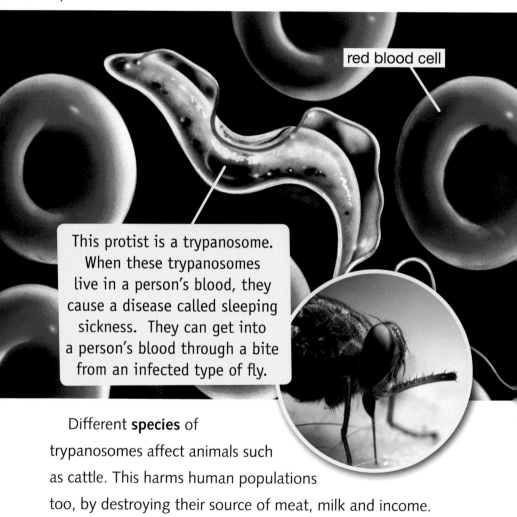

red blood cell

This protist is a trypanosome. When these trypanosomes live in a person's blood, they cause a disease called sleeping sickness. They can get into a person's blood through a bite from an infected type of fly.

Different **species** of trypanosomes affect animals such as cattle. This harms human populations too, by destroying their source of meat, milk and income.

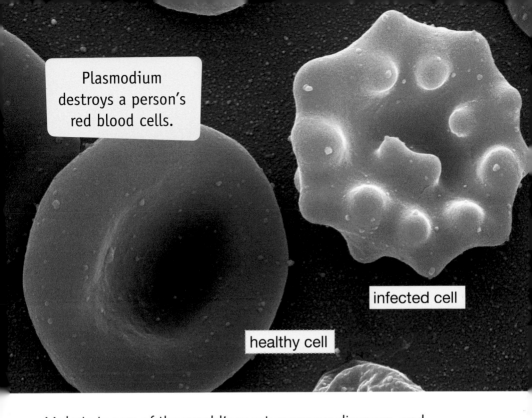

Plasmodium destroys a person's red blood cells.

infected cell

healthy cell

Malaria is one of the world's most common diseases, and one of the world's biggest killers. It's caused by a tiny protist called Plasmodium. Plasmodium enters a person's body when an infected mosquito bites them. This means it's most common in tropical areas of the world where these mosquitoes live, such as sub-Saharan Africa. Around 40% of malaria deaths occur in Nigeria and the Democratic Republic of the Congo.

MICRO STATS

Cases of malaria every year: **207,000,000**
People killed by malaria every year: **627,000**

# Masters of disguise

Protists cause such deadly diseases because they are good at hiding from our immune systems. Trypanosomes are masters of disguise. They can change their outer "coat", which is the part that our white blood cells use to recognise invaders. Trypanosomes change their coats so often, our white blood cells can't keep up.

Plasmodium tricks our immune system by living inside our liver cells and red blood cells. This helps it to survive and reproduce, but it makes sufferers horribly ill.

**The Plasmodium life cycle**

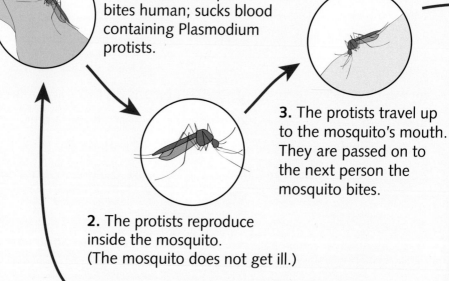

**1.** (Female) mosquito bites human; sucks blood containing Plasmodium protists.

**3.** The protists travel up to the mosquito's mouth. They are passed on to the next person the mosquito bites.

**2.** The protists reproduce inside the mosquito. (The mosquito does not get ill.)

**5.** If the person is bitten by a mosquito, the cycle begins again.

# Insect carriers

Many protist parasites have complicated life cycles, which makes them hard to fight. Plasmodium spends part of its life inside mosquitoes. It's almost impossible to control the mosquitoes, which makes it very difficult to control malaria. The different stages of the Plasmodium life cycle also make it hard to develop medicines for malaria, but there are ways to treat the disease if the symptoms are spotted early enough.

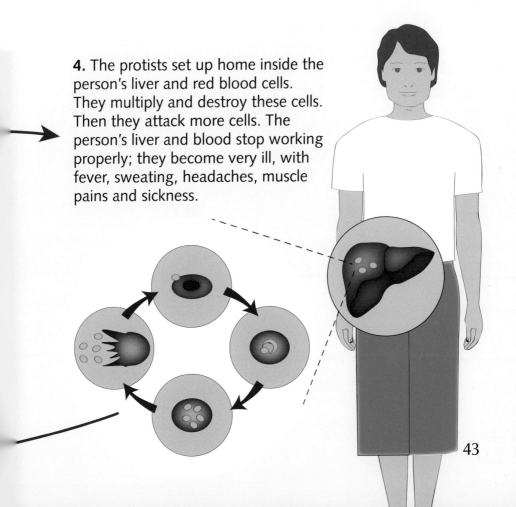

**4.** The protists set up home inside the person's liver and red blood cells. They multiply and destroy these cells. Then they attack more cells. The person's liver and blood stop working properly; they become very ill, with fever, sweating, headaches, muscle pains and sickness.

# Plant pests

Protists can also cause disease in plants. The main culprits are slime moulds and water moulds. They are called moulds because scientists once thought they were types of fungi. Like fungi, these protists get their energy by breaking down organic materials. When they do this on a living plant, they can damage the plant or even kill it.

This tomato plant is infected with a water mould. Once infected, the whole vine rots away in less than 14 days.

Slime moulds can clump together as a gooey mass of microorganisms, which creeps slowly along the ground like a strange slug! They actually eat bacteria, but they can damage plants by blocking the sun and air.

Water moulds also reproduce by making spores, just like fungi. Spores can travel through water, so water moulds spread quickly in wet weather. When they start growing on plants, they can rot the leaves, stems or roots. Sometimes they stop fruits or vegetables growing properly, or leave patches of damage that make them inedible. Sometimes they kill the plant altogether.

# The Irish potato famine

In the late 1840s, a plant disease called blight destroyed Ireland's entire potato crop. Potatoes were the main source of food and income in Ireland at the time, so this caused a famine that lasted for 15 years. In Ireland alone, a million people died of starvation or illness because their bodies were so weak. Another 1.5 million people left Ireland to live in different countries. This had a devastating impact on a country with a population of just 8 million.

The poorest people suffered most, because they relied on home-grown potatoes for food, and had no money to buy other things to eat.

Blight rots the roots and tubers of potato plants.

The culprit was a tiny protist called Phytophthora infestans. This water mould infects the leaves, stems and roots of potato plants. It feeds by releasing chemicals that digest the surface it's living on into smaller pieces that the protist can take in. As the protist feeds, the potatoes are broken down into slimy black gunk.

## How blight spreads

Like all water moulds, blight spreads quickly in cool, damp weather. After the disease first appeared, farmers left the rotten potatoes in the field. This helped the disease to spread. But it wasn't just heavy rains and blight that were to blame for the Irish potato famine. Food was imported from other countries, but it was not distributed properly to the poorest people.

# Viruses

Viruses are the tiniest microorganisms. Each flu virus is about a billionth of a metre wide, which means that hundreds of thousands can fit inside one human cell.

## Are viruses alive or not?

Viruses are not cells. Scientists aren't sure if viruses really count as living things. A virus stranded in soil or lying on a table doesn't feed, grow, move or reproduce. But if it gets inside a living cell, it springs into action.

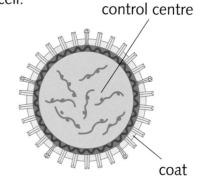

control centre

coat

Viruses are just little control centres, protected by a tough coat.

These tiny viruses are attacking a much bigger bacterium.

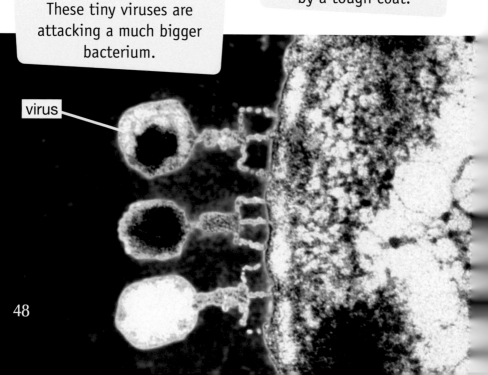

virus

Some viruses are shaped like rods or spheres. Others are polyhedrons – shapes with a certain number of sides.

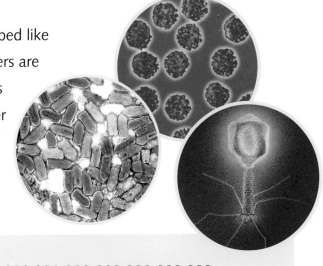

# MOST WANTED

**Dimitri Ivanovsky (1864-1920),
Friedrich Loeffler (1852-1915)
Paul Frosch (1860-1928)**

Nobody knew about viruses until 1892, when Dimitri Ivanovsky tried to work out what was causing a disease in tobacco plants. He discovered that it was something much smaller than bacteria. In 1898, Friedrich Loeffler and Paul Frosch noticed the same for foot-and-mouth disease in animals. These mysterious microorganisms became known as viruses.

# How viruses work

In the right conditions, living cells can reproduce. Look back at the pictures of bacteria, fungi and protist cells. They are packed with equipment for making copies of themselves. Each one has a control centre, which tells the rest of the cell what do to.

This is how a flu virus infects cells in your nose and throat:

Each cell can make thousands of copies of a virus before it bursts, so the infection spreads quickly.

**1.** A virus drifts along and sticks to a cell.

virus

cell

**6.** The new viruses infect new host cells, and the cycle starts again.

**5.** The new viruses leave the host cell. Sometimes they break out by making the cell explode. This kills the cell.

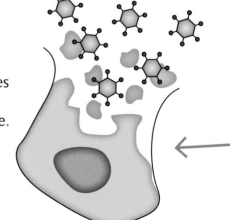

Viruses are different – they only have the control centre. Viruses can only reproduce if they can get inside a living cell – the cell of a plant, animal, fungi, bacteria or protist. Once inside, the virus tricks the host cell into doing all the hard work!

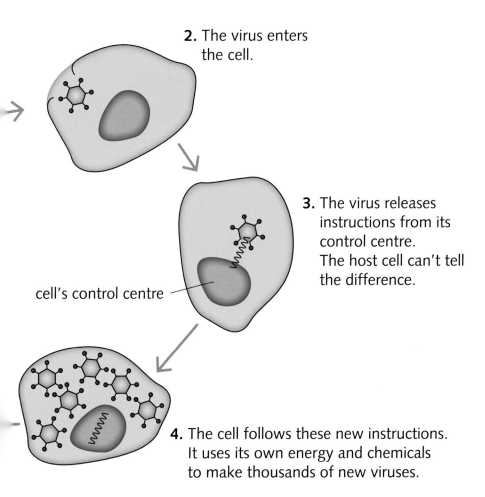

**2.** The virus enters the cell.

**3.** The virus releases instructions from its control centre. The host cell can't tell the difference.

cell's control centre

**4.** The cell follows these new instructions. It uses its own energy and chemicals to make thousands of new viruses.

# Villainous viruses

Hijacking cells and making them explode is exactly how viruses make us ill. Your immune system can spot human cells that have been infected by a virus, and destroy them. But this takes time. Before it happens, the virus may damage so many cells that we start to feel ill.

More than 220 viruses are known to cause disease in humans, and three or four new ones are found every year. Some viruses – such as the ones that cause colds – only infect one part of our bodies, and are beaten by our immune systems very quickly. Others – such as measles and mumps – infect cells in many different parts of our bodies. They are harder for our bodies to fight, and they make us feel much worse.

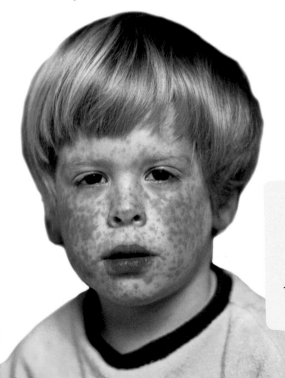

A virus causes measles. It has been infecting people around the world for more than 1000 years.

# How viruses spread

Most common viruses, such as the ones that cause colds, flu, measles or chicken pox, are eventually beaten by our immune systems. To survive, they need to move to a new host.

Some viruses spread very easily. People infected with cold and flu viruses produce lots of mucus. Each time they sneeze, thousands of tiny droplets are sprayed into the air. Each one is packed with viruses. If another person breathes them in, they will begin to attack that person's cells. Other viruses, such as Ebola virus, can only spread through direct contact.

Each droplet of mucus is packed with viruses.

# Case study:

# Ebola virus

Ebola virus first infected humans in 1976. It is one of the deadliest human viruses. It usually lives inside the bodies of fruit bats, and does them no harm. But when Ebola gets inside a human, it attacks the cells that line a patient's blood vessels. This means it affects many parts of the patient's body at the same time, and often kills.

Doctors and nurses need to wear protective masks and gloves when they treat patients with Ebola, because the virus can get into the body through the eyes, nose and tiny cuts on the skin.

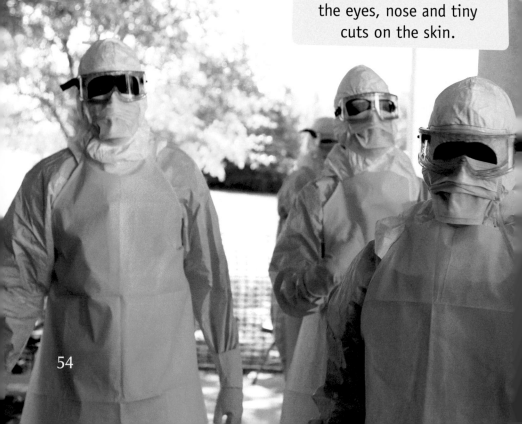

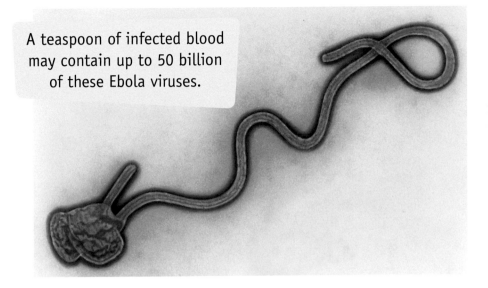

A teaspoon of infected blood may contain up to 50 billion of these Ebola viruses.

An infected person has Ebola virus in their blood, sweat and other body fluids. If another person touches the patient, or their bedding or clothing, the virus may get into their body too. This is how Ebola spreads.

## An Ebola epidemic

The largest-ever Ebola outbreak began in March 2014, in Guinea. It spread so far and so fast, that it became an epidemic. Thousands of people died. When the epidemic began, there were no medicines to treat Ebola. The only way to stop the epidemic was to prevent people from getting infected. This included teaching people how the disease spreads, so they could keep themselves safe. Scientists are also working hard to invent and test medicines to treat Ebola.

# From virus to vaccination

Once your body has beaten a virus, you're unlikely to be infected by it again – even if the virus gets inside you. You become immune to the disease. Your body learns to recognise that virus, and destroy it quickly before it can make you ill.

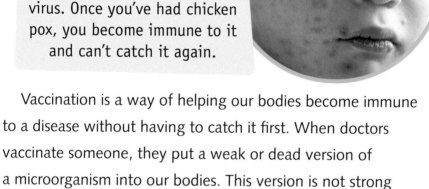

Chicken pox is caused by a virus. Once you've had chicken pox, you become immune to it and can't catch it again.

Vaccination is a way of helping our bodies become immune to a disease without having to catch it first. When doctors vaccinate someone, they put a weak or dead version of a microorganism into our bodies. This version is not strong enough to make us ill, but it teaches our immune system to recognise and fight the real thing.

Children are given vaccinations to teach their bodies how to fight many dangerous viruses, including measles and polio. There are vaccinations for diseases caused by bacteria and fungi too.

# How vaccines work

A weakened form of the pathogen is injected into the body. The body makes white blood cells that can recognize and fight the pathogen. If the real pathogen ever enters the body, the immune system is ready to fight it immediately.

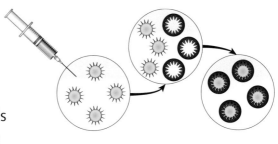

# MOST WANTED

Edward Jenner invented vaccination, to fight a deadly virus called smallpox. For thousands of years, smallpox affected people in every corner of the world. It killed one in every three sufferers, and left survivors with horrible scars. Jenner tried infecting a boy with cowpox virus to see if it would teach his body to fight smallpox. Luckily for Jenner – and the boy – it worked! No one in the world catches smallpox anymore. It was the first disease to be completely stamped out by vaccination.

**Edward Jenner**
(1749–1823)

# Germ wars

As humans learn more about microorganisms, we get better at protecting ourselves from their harmful effects. Today's doctors have many different methods to prevent and treat diseases caused by bacteria, viruses, protists and fungi. Our most powerful medicines were only developed in the last 100 years.

## Killer chemicals

Long before they knew that microorganisms existed, people were using antiseptics to stop the spread of disease. Antiseptics are chemicals that can kill or stop the growth or many kinds of microorganisms. Some plants produce natural antiseptics to protect themselves from attack. They were the source of the first antiseptics.

Things like antiseptics, bleach and boiling water are very good at killing microbes outside the body. But they couldn't be used inside the body because they damage human cells too!

Thousands of years ago, people discovered that a tree sap called frankincense helped to heal wounds.

# MOST WANTED

## Florence Nightingale
(1820–1910)

In the 1800s, hospitals were like holiday camps for bacteria. All those people living and working together made it easy for bacteria to spread. Florence Nightingale helped to change this when she introduced measures like hand washing and cleaning to hospitals. She didn't know about germs – she just knew that keeping hospitals, equipment and patients clean could help prevent diseases. Her methods soon spread around the world.

# Antibiotics

In the last 100 years, scientists have developed medicines that can fight microorganisms inside our bodies. The most famous are antibiotics – medicines that can harm or destroy bacteria.

## Germ versus germ!

The first antibiotics were made using Penicillium mould – a type of fungus that grows on bread and fruit in our homes. In 1928, Alexander Fleming discovered that this mould produces a substance that can kill lots of different types of bacteria. The mould does this to protect itself from attacks by bacteria.

Fleming thought it would be brilliant if we could harness this power to help people. Fleming's famous discovery was an accident – he was growing bacteria in petri dishes, and left them to go mouldy. When he picked up one of the dishes, he noticed the mould had killed all the bacteria.

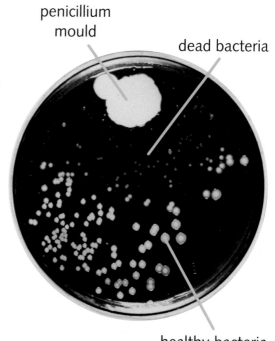

penicillium mould

dead bacteria

healthy bacteria

# From mould to medicine

In the 1940s, Howard Florey and Ernst Chain worked out how to get Penicillium mould to grow more quickly, and how to extract enough of the bacteria-fighting substance to make medicine. Doctors finally had a medicine that was great at killing bacteria and didn't harm patients.

Even really nasty bacterial infections, such as tetanus and pneumonia, could now be cured. Penicillin also made surgery much safer.

# MOST WANTED

**Dorothy Hodgkin**
(1910–1994)

Dorothy Hodgkin discovered exactly how penicillin was made up. This helped scientists to understand how it worked, so they could create new antibiotics. During the 19th century, thousands more antibiotics were made. Many came from soil bacteria that produce strong antibiotics to fend off attack from their neighbours!

# Antibiotic resistance

At first antibiotics seemed like a miracle cure for the many diseases caused by bacteria. But bacteria began fighting back.

Bacteria reproduce very quickly. This means they can adapt very quickly to changes in their habitat. Imagine a population of bacteria living inside a person. If the person takes antibiotics, the habitat suddenly becomes dangerous for bacteria.

The antibiotic starts to kill the bacteria – but it can't kill them all. This is because no two bacteria are exactly the same. Small differences or variation between the bacteria means that the antibiotic will not affect some of them. These bacteria are resistant to antibiotics. Most of the bacteria are killed, but resistant bacteria survive.

The resistant bacteria now have all the food and space to themselves. They reproduce, and pass on their resistance. Soon the only bacteria left are the antibiotic-resistant type. The population of bacteria has adapted to the new habitat. Doctors find it very difficult to treat infections caused by antibiotic-resistant bacteria, so they can be deadly.

Every time we take antibiotics, we change the habitat inside our bodies and give bacteria a chance to become resistant. It's important to take antibiotics only when you really need them, and not for illnesses caused by viruses. Antibiotics can only fight bacteria – they can't fight viruses.

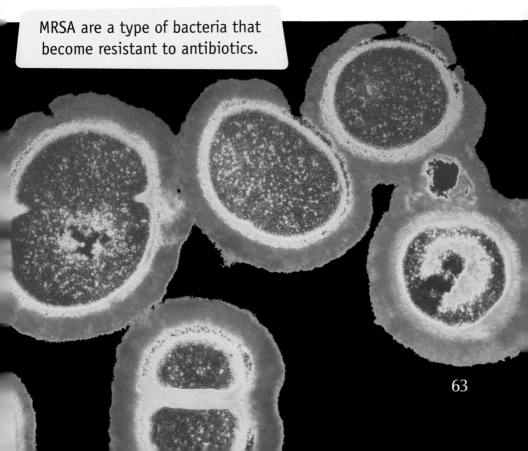

MRSA are a type of bacteria that become resistant to antibiotics.

# New weapons

It is getting harder to find or make new antibiotics. Doctors worry that more and more bacteria will become resistant. So scientists are exploring new ways to fight bacteria – using viruses.

# Attack of the phages

Viruses don't just infect plants and animals. There are viruses that infect bacteria too. Scientists discovered these "phages" more than a hundred years ago.

 **MICRO STATS** 1 billion Phages in a millilitre of river water
1 million Bacteria in a millilitre of river water

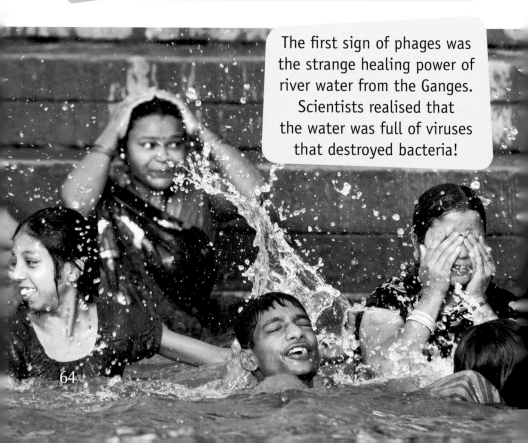

The first sign of phages was the strange healing power of river water from the Ganges. Scientists realised that the water was full of viruses that destroyed bacteria!

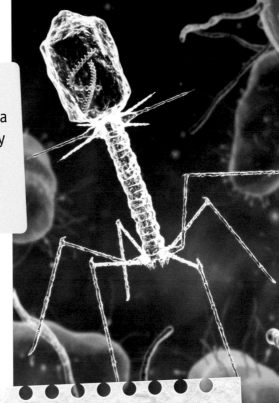

"Phages" look like little spacecraft. They hijack bacteria and get them to make so many new viruses, they explode! The new viruses go on to infect more bacteria.

Scientists are trying to find out if phages are a good way to kill disease-causing bacteria in our bodies.

| Pros | Cons |
|---|---|
| Phages only attack bacteria, so they don't affect human cells. | Need to find different phages for each type of bacteria. |
| Easy to find new types – phages are everywhere! | Our immune systems might fight and kill the phages. |
| Each phage only attacks one type of bacteria, so it won't harm friendly bacteria in the body. | Patients might not like being injected with a virus. |
| Phages have been used to treat patients in Russia, Georgia and Poland for many years. | Bacteria could adapt to become resistant to phages |

# Big ideas

Scientists still don't know everything about microorganisms. The more we find out the more we can use them to help people.

# Divide and conquer

Scientists are studying how bacteria form huge sticky colonies called biofilms. You might find biofilms forming around taps or plugholes that haven't been cleaned for a while. They are made up of millions of bacteria, protected by a slimy coating.

Sticking together in a biofilm helps bacteria to survive in all sorts of places. It also helps protect them from medicines such as antibiotics. By finding out how biofilms are formed, scientists hope to find new ways to stop so many bacteria from growing in one place. One idea is to cover hospital furniture and equipment in tiny bumps, disrupting the surfaces that bacteria grow on.

This is a close-up of the biofilm of bacteria living around the drain of a clean kitchen sink!

bacterium

slimy coating

A Colorado potato beetle devouring a leaf. Without leaves, the plant can't make its own food and the crop will fail.

## Pest control

As well as fighting each other, microorganisms can be used to fight much bigger pests – such as insects. Viruses and fungi have been used to control certain beetles that destroy crops. Because they are natural, they are more environmentally friendly than **insecticides**.

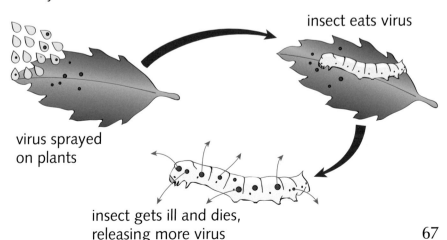

insect eats virus

virus sprayed on plants

insect gets ill and dies, releasing more virus

# Harnessing micro-powers!

Humans have found hundreds of ways to harness the natural power of bacteria, fungi, protists and viruses, and make them work for us. You'll find microorganisms doing useful jobs everywhere from supermarkets to sewage works.

## Cleaning water

Humans produce a lot of waste – not least from our own bodies. In the UK alone, 250,000 toilets are flushed every minute! All this dirty water flows to sewage works. Apart from bad smells, there doesn't seem to be much action at a sewage treatment plant. But zoom in, and you'd see millions of microorganisms hard at work, cleaning wastewater from our baths, sinks and toilets so we can use it again.

# Waste munchers

Microbiologists have found types of bacteria that can break down crude oil, plastic bags and even methane (a global warming gas). Bacteria may be able to help solve big environmental problems in the future. For example, oil-munching bacteria, rather than chemicals, may be used to clean up oil spills.

Microbes do many different jobs at a sewage treatment plant.

**1** Bacteria feed on dangerous substances dissolved in the water, breaking them down into safe and useful minerals.

**2** Protists hunt and eat bacteria, removing them from the water.

**3** Protists are big enough to be filtered out of the water later in the process)

**4** Many different microorganisms break down the leftover sludge.

**5** By the end, the water is clean enough to be put into a river!

69

## Making dinner

Microorganisms don't just break substances down. As they go about their normal lives, they also produce all sorts of new substances. Some of these are very useful – especially for making food.

## The yoghurt-makers

Bacteria are used to turn milk into thick and creamy yoghurt. The bacteria feed on sugars in the milk. As they break the sugars down, they produce an acid that makes the milk thicker. Substances produced by the bacteria also give yoghurt its special tangy taste. Using different species of bacteria can create very different yoghurts!

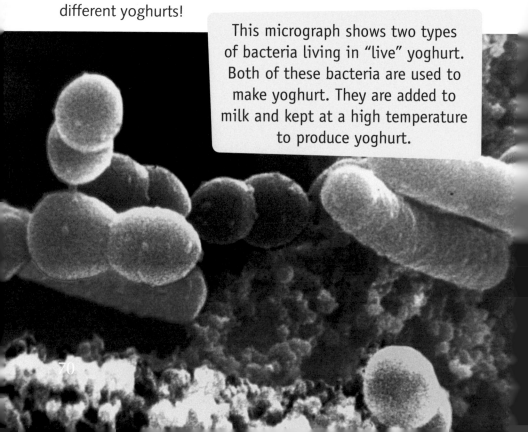

This micrograph shows two types of bacteria living in "live" yoghurt. Both of these bacteria are used to make yoghurt. They are added to milk and kept at a high temperature to produce yoghurt.

In a yoghurt factory, fermentation takes place in huge vats. The temperature has to be just right – at 42°C – for the bacteria to do their job.

The process is called fermentation, because the bacteria are breaking down the milk sugars without using air. Fermentation only happens when the bacteria are nice and warm. When the yoghurt is ready, it is cooled down to stop the bacteria. Sometimes yoghurt is heated after fermentation to kill the bacteria, but "live" yoghurt still contains the living bacteria. These bacteria are harmless to eat, and may actually be very good for us. Extra "friendly bacteria" may also be added to yoghurt, to help to keep our digestive systems healthy.

Microorganisms are used to make many other foods too.
Look out for these microbe-power products on your plate!

Yeast is used to make bread. This fungus feeds on sugar, burping out a gas called carbon dioxide. Bubbles of gas collect in the dough, making it rise. Baking the bread makes the bubbles bigger, and traps them so the bread is light and spongey.

Acid-producing bacteria are used to make cheese as well as yoghurt. Moulds (a type of fungi) are added to some cheeses, to give them special, strong flavours.

You'll find citric acid listed on thousands of food labels. This wonder-chemical is used to preserve everything from sweets to shampoo. Most of the world's citric acid is produced by a fungus. For the fungus, citric acid is just a waste product made as it feeds on sugar.

Even algae are used to make food! A gloopy goo made by brown algae and some bacteria is used to thicken foods such as jam and ice cream, and stop them from going bad.

Xanthan gum is used to thicken sauces, and give other foods a nice texture. It's made by bacteria – the same bacteria that make rotting vegetables go slimy!

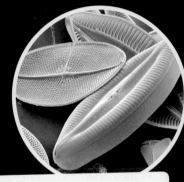

You'll need to brush your teeth after all that food! And for that you'll need diatoms. These tiny algae are used to make toothpaste. Their hard glassy shells are perfect for scraping sticky bacteria off our teeth.

# Harmful or helpful?

Bacteria, fungi, protists and viruses are everywhere. About 400 trillion of these microscopic creatures are having a party in your body right now!

But even if we could rid the world – and ourselves – of microorganisms, would we want to?

Some cause deadly diseases, but most are essential for life on Earth. They break down dead plants and animals, and recycle the nutrients that all living things need to grow and survive. We give some of them a place to live, and in return they help keep us alive. The mysterious world of microorganisms is also our world.

## Know your neighbours

Since scientists worked out how bacteria, fungi, protists and viruses cause harm, many diseases have become treatable, curable or even wiped out altogether. Understanding the useful things microbes do is important too. It helps us put microbes to work – as medicines, decomposers or living factories.

# MOST WANTED

# YOU!

Scientists who study bacteria, viruses, fungi and protists are called microbiologists. It's an exciting area to work in. Microbiologists might find themselves collecting samples from volcanoes or rainforests, or making world-changing discoveries in the lab. If you are curious and creative, you could become a microbiologist and unlock more secrets of this mysterious world.

# Glossary

**absorb**      take in

**adapt**      when a population of living things changes over time, to become better suited to their habitat

**antiseptic**      chemical that stops microorganisms from growing

**carbohydrate**      substance such as sugar, starch and cellulose, that contain carbon, hydrogen and oxygen. Can be broken down by many living things to release energy.

**carbon**      substance that is found in most living things

**cell**      smallest building block of a living thing

**coma**      long period of unconsciousness

**contaminate**      make something dirty or polluted by adding something to it

**decomposing**      becoming rotten, causing something to decay

**decomposer**      living thing that can cause decay

**diabetes**      illness where a person's body cannot store sugar properly

**electron microscope**      microscope that can magnify an object millions of times, using beams of electrons instead of light

**enamel**      hard, white substance that covers our teeth

**epidemic**      when a disease spreads to many people or animals at once

**estimate**      best guess

**filter**      pass a liquid through certain materials, to remove solid particles

**flagella**      tiny, whip-like "tail" which some microorganisms use to swim

**fungicide**    chemical that kills fungi

**germinate**    start to grow

**immune**    resistant to a disease, because your body has already learned how to fight it

**insecticide**    chemical that kills insects, or stops them from growing

**multiply**    increase in number

**nitrogen**    substance that is found in most living things

**nutrient**    substance that is essential for a living thing to survive and grow

**pickling**    keeping something in a strong acid such as vinegar to kill any microorganisms and stop or slow down decay

**plankton**    tiny living things, including microorganisms, that drift or float in seas, rivers or lakes, and provide food for larger animals

**plaque**    sticky layer on teeth, where many bacteria live

**population**    living things in a particular place

**reproduce**    make copes of themselves

**resistant**    not affected by antibiotics

**species**    group of living things that are so similar, they can reproduce

**symptom**    sign of disease that can be seen or felt by the patient

**toxic**    poisonous

**variation**    small differences between living thing of the same type

**white blood cell**    cells found in our blood, that help our bodies to fight invading microorganisms

# Your micro-sized neighbours

Microorganisms are used to make lifesaving medicines, such as antibiotics.

Microorganisms munch on our sewage to break it down, cleaning the water so we can use it again.

You brush away bacteria when you clean your teeth!

Biofilms of bacteria form around plugholes.

Cut flowers will eventually rot as bacteria and fungi break them down for food.

Algae in the ocean produced most of the oxygen you are breathing!

Most pillows are filled with tiny fungi, which can cause problems for people with asthma.

Viruses, protists and bacteria may be tiny, but they can make us very ill.

Many foods, from yoghurt to tomato ketchup, are made using microorganisms.

Keeping food cold stops bacteria and fungi from breaking it down quickly.

Without the microorganisms in a cow's stomach, there would be no milk!

Cooking food can kill harmful bacteria.

# Ideas for reading

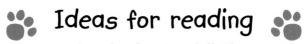

Written by Clare Dowdall, PhD
Lecturer and Primary Literacy Consultant

**Reading objectives:**
- check that the book makes sense to them, discussing their understanding and exploring the meaning of words in context
- ask questions to improve their understanding
- summarise the main ideas drawn from more than one paragraph, identifying key details that support the main ideas
- retrieve and record information from non-fiction

**Spoken language objectives:**
- ask relevant questions to extend their understanding and knowledge

**Curriculum links: Science** – living things and their habitats

**Resources:** art materials for posters; ICT for research

## Build a context for reading
- Ask children to suggest what they think a microorganism is. Collect their ideas on a whiteboard as a spider-diagram.
- Read the title together, help children to notice that the title contains a prefix micro. Discuss what this prefix means and ask for examples of other words that contain it, e.g. microphone, microscope, microchip.
- Read the blurb and check that children understand that microorganisms are tiny organisms, undetectable to the human eye. Check also that they know what an organism is (a living thing).

## Understand and apply reading strategies
- Turn to the contents. Using this and the spider-diagram information, help children to prepare further for reading by making a list of questions in pairs about microorganisms that they will explore through reading.
- Consider the final chapter heading "Harmful or Helpful". Discuss what this implies and whether the children think that there are more harmful or helpful microorganisms.